PURSUING *Purpose*
WITH DR. PEARL

www.PearlPugh.com

Hey There! I'm EXCITED about Your Release. Thank You for Trusting the God in Me to Walk with You on this Journey. I know it's not easy but YOU are worth it. IT IS WELL! This is Your Season, Walk in it! Live Out Loud and RELEASE. Trust God through the Process and You Will Win.

Love You On Purpose,
Dr. Pearl Pugh

Copyright 2023
All rights reserved to Dr. Pearl Pugh.
Content illustration licensed and subject
to copyright. No part of this publication is
legal to duplicate,
reproduced, or transmitted in any form or by
any means,
including photocopying, recording, or any
other electronic
or mechanical method without written
permission
of Dr. Pearl Pugh.

THIS JOURNAL
Belongs to:

_____
_____
_____
_____

Do not be anxious about anything, but in every situation, by prayer and petition, with thanksgiving, present your requests to God. And the peace of God, which transcends all understanding, will guard your hearts and your minds in Christ Jesus.
Psalm 34:4–5, 8

When You Desire To Walk In Your God-Given Purpose, and You Take Both Spiritual and Practical Steps Toward Becoming The Person You're Called To Be and Doing The Things You're Called To Do, It Changes Everything... From The Inside Out.

Your Purpose

This book returns the overlap to 'purpose' and uses the four questions to help you explore your passion, mission, vocation and profession so you can put into words your life purpose.

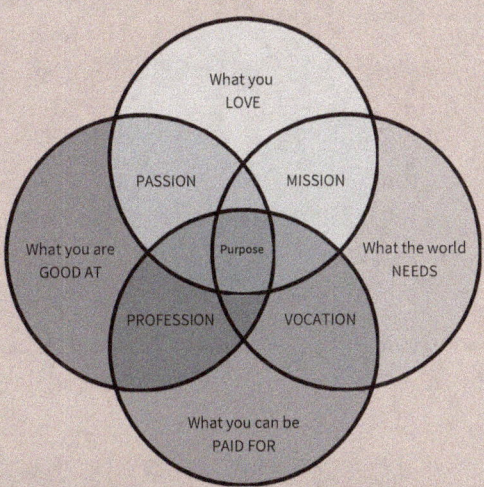

Purpose is not a life goal to achieve. It is not a framework to measure or test yourself against. It is a daily practice to feel good. You have a destiny that will bring glory to God, share the grace of God, and extend the reign of God.

Why should you have purpose?
Having zest for living and joy in life can increase your tendency to care for yourself, such as eating well, doing moderate exercise, feeling wanted and needed, having enjoyable social connections. These practices can improve overall health including mental health, and reduce fatigue and stress-related illnesses such as heart disease. Understanding your unique destiny starts with understanding what the Bible says about your purpose as one of God's people.

How do you find your purpose?
Clarifying what the Bible says about your purpose helps you in three important ways:
- It declares why you exist. It captures the heart of why you are on this earth and why Jesus died for you.
- It defines your life—not in terms of what you think but what God thinks. It anchors your life in the character and call of God.
- It clarifies the non-negotiables. It identifies what never changes about who you are, regardless of circumstances.

Exploring Human Needs

A vital part of finding your purpose is understanding that all humans have similar needs that drive us. The way we meet them is different for everyone. Living on purpose can help to meet many of these needs, and understanding how to meet them for ourselves is important to understanding our purpose. Many teachers have outlined these eight:

- Life satisfaction
- Change and growth
- A bright future
- Resonance
- Freedom
- Self-actualisation
- Meaning and value
- Sense of purpose

This workbook helps you explore these needs, and recognize that while we may not have the answers, we can give ourselves the freedom to reflect on and explore them.

When should you start looking?

Many people believe that humans don't make major changes until they're at the lowest point of their lives: a crisis point. Which isn't a fun place to get to, or to be.

But change is possible without the crisis - you simply need to choose to change.

Getting the most from this workbook

Read through the workbook. At each stage ask yourself the questions proposed, and give yourself the priority to explore some possible responses.

By the time you've worked all the way through, you could have a clearer sense of your purpose.

Remember though, it's a journey and a practice, something you do each day. Give yourself as much time as you need to reach clarity.

Tips:

Finding Your Purpose In Christ

- Keep yourself in God's Word
- Surround yourself with wise counselors
- Pray for wisdom and discernment
- Prioritize doing God's will
- Pay attention to your passions

The Power of Prayer

KEY VERSE: _____
_____

"Trust in the Lord with all your heart and lean not on your own understanding." - Proverbs 3:5

DEVOTIONAL

Embracing God's Unconditional Love
Reflect on the depth of God's love for you, knowing that His love is not based on your performance but on His grace and mercy. Seek to understand and experience the vastness of His unconditional love.

MAIN POINTS

- God's love for us is not based on our performance but on His grace.
- We can experience the depth of God's unconditional love in our lives.

Reflect on a time when you experienced God's unconditional love in your life. How did it impact you and your relationship with Him?

PRAYER

Your Purpose Diagram

- What you LOVE
- What the world NEEDS
- What you can be PAID FOR
- What you are GOOD AT
- PASSION
- MISSION
- VOCATION
- PROFESSION
- **Purpose**

Exploring the Character of Jesus

KEY VERSE: _____
_____

"I can do all things through Christ who strengthens me."
- Philippians 4:13

DEVOTIONAL

Commit your plans and decisions to the Lord, seeking His guidance and wisdom in all areas of your life. Trust that He will lead you on the right path as you surrender to His will.

MAIN POINTS

- ○ God is our source of wisdom and guidance in all areas of life.
- ○ **Trusting in God's guidance leads us to the right path and brings peace.**

PRAYER

In what area of your life do you need God's guidance the most right now? Take time to pray and seek His wisdom and direction.

Why Are You Looking For Your Purpose Right Now?

Who Do You Know That Seems to Already Be Living Their Purpose?

This might be someone you know, or someone you admire like a teacher or a celebrity. Name them and what their purpose seems to be.

Name	Their purpose

Finding and Facing My Blocks

We all have emotions. They can be so intense that researchers have studied them over generations. They drive much of our behaviour. The list below is the nine core emotions (and their secondary cousins) that are common to all humans, regardless of age, gender, race or religion.

When you think about finding your purpose, what feelings might stop or distract you? Circle any that might come up for you. In the next step you'll look at how you'll process them.

Anger	Fear	Pain
Resentment	Apprehension	Hurt
Irritation	Overwhelmed	Pity
Frustration	Threatened	Sad
Annoyance	Concern	Shock
Exasperation	Dread	Despair

Joy	Passion	Love
Happy	Enthusiasm	Affection
Elated	Desire	Tenderness
Hopeful	Zest	Compassion
Peace	Zeal	Warmth
Pleasure	Eagerness	Fondness

Shame	Guilt	Loneliness
Embarrassment	Regretful	Abandoned
Humble	Contrite	Estranged
Disgraced	Remorseful	Rejected
Exposed	Erring	Isolated
Unworthy	Sorrowful	Forlorn

How to Deal with These Emotions When They Come Up

Understanding what we're feeling when we're feeling it, and being able to respond in the way we prefer, is called emotional intelligence (EQ). For most people, developing EQ is a life-long quest. Regardless of where you are on your EQ journey, reflect here on how you choose to deal with the emotions you outlined on the previous page, as they come up for you while you're seeking your own answers.

_____
_____
_____
_____
_____
_____
_____
_____
_____
_____
_____
_____
_____
_____
_____
_____
_____
_____
_____
_____
_____

What Jobs Do People In Your Family Always Do? And 'Not Do'?

Some families have many health professionals, some have many tradespeople, some are teachers, some have many different jobs. Think about your wider family when answering this. Keep writing until you run out of people.

Which of these jobs are interesting to you? Rank them 1-5, with 1 being not interesting, and 5 being very interesting.

Job	Ranking

The Importance of *Faith*

KEY VERSE: _____
_____

"Be still, and know that I am God." - Psalm 46:10

DEVOTIONAL

Discover the power of God's Word as a source of strength and encouragement. Spend time reading and meditating on Scripture, allowing it to transform your thoughts and renew your spirit.

MAIN POINTS

- ○ The Word of God is powerful and transformative.
- ○ Spending time in God's Word strengthens our faith and renews our minds.

Choose a verse from the Bible that brings you comfort and strength. Reflect on its meaning and how it can apply to your current situation.

PRAYER

Why Are You Looking For Your Purpose Right Now?

What are Human Needs?

We are all driven by basic needs. They motivate our actions. Knowing or feeling that you need something (even if you don't quite know what it is) does not make you weak or needy, it makes you human. Whether we know it or not, these needs drive every decision.

Explore these in the next section.

- Life Satisfaction
- Change and Growth
- A Bright Future
- Connection
- Freedom
- Self-Actualization
- Meaning and Value
- Sense of Purpose

Life Satisfaction

What in your life helps you feel satisfied? It might be an aspect of a job, a course of study, a hobby, or relationships. List them all here. The list doesn't need any structure - just write.

_____
_____
_____
_____
_____
_____
_____
_____
_____
_____
_____
_____

What reduces your feelings of satisfaction with life?

_____
_____
_____
_____
_____
_____
_____
_____
_____
_____
_____
_____
_____

Change and Growth

Where has your life become stale? List all the areas here. The list doesn't need any structure - just write.

_____
_____
_____
_____
_____
_____
_____
_____
_____
_____
_____
_____

For each of these areas, what could you change now? In a month? In six months? In a year?

_____
_____
_____
_____
_____
_____
_____
_____
_____
_____
_____
_____

Unveiling the Meaning of Grace and *Salvation*

KEY VERSE: _____

"For I know the plans I have for you," declares the Lord, "plans to prosper you and not to harm you, plans to give you hope and a future." - Jeremiah 29:11

DEVOTIONAL

Set aside time to rest in God's presence, allowing Him to quiet your soul and bring you peace. Find solace in His comforting embrace and experience His restorative power.

MAIN POINTS

- In God's presence, we find rest and peace for our souls.
- Resting in God's presence brings restoration and rejuvenation.

PRAYER

Create a quiet and peaceful space where you can spend time in God's presence. Describe how you feel when you intentionally set aside time to rest and connect with Him.

A Bright Future

What do you want to show up in your life this week? This month? This year? The list doesn't need any structure - just write.

_____
_____
_____
_____
_____
_____
_____
_____
_____
_____
_____
_____
_____
_____
_____
_____
_____
_____
_____
_____
_____
_____
_____
_____
_____
_____
_____
_____

Connection

What people do you feel connected to? Also describe how you feel connected to them. The list doesn't need any structure - just write.

Freedom

This is about freedom of choice. It may even be about choosing to sacrifice freedom now for the promise of freedom in the future - like working a 9-to-5 job now for the promise of an abundant retirement. The list doesn't need any structure - just write.

Self Actualization

What personal mission are or do you want to pursue, that you feel is unique to you? This covers everything from writing a book on the history of Africa to discovering a new star.

_____
_____
_____
_____
_____
_____
_____
_____
_____
_____
_____
_____
_____
_____
_____
_____
_____
_____
_____
_____
_____
_____

Understanding the Role of the Holy Spirit

KEY VERSE: _____

_____

"The Lord is my strength and my shield; my heart trusts in him, and he helps me." - Psalm 28:7

DEVOTIONAL

Release your worries and anxieties to the Lord, knowing that He cares for you. Trust in His faithfulness and ability to carry your burdens, and experience the freedom that comes from placing your trust in Him.

MAIN POINTS

- God cares for us and invites us to cast our anxieties on Him.
- **Surrendering our worries to God allows us to experience His peace and provision.**

PRAYER

Write down your current worries and anxieties. Spend time in prayer, surrendering each one to God and asking Him to replace your worries with His peace.

Meaning and Value

We may not have the answers, but can give ourselves the freedom to reflect on and explore them.

What am I living for? Or by whom am I needed?

_____
_____
_____
_____
_____

What is a life goal unique to me? Am I doing my best to achieve it?

_____
_____
_____
_____
_____

Overall, do I deserve to exist?

_____
_____
_____
_____
_____

In general, is life worth living?

_____
_____
_____
_____
_____

Sense of Purpose

There are three main ways to discover your personal mission: by fate leading you there, by personal interest, or making a conscious choice based on life experience. This could be a quiet achievement, it doesn't mean being the CEO or the most influential influencer. It's understanding the bigger picture of your life.

Discovering God's Promises and Their *Relevance*

KEY VERSE: _____
_____

"Do not be anxious about anything, but in every situation, by prayer and petition, with thanksgiving, present your requests to God." - Philippians 4:6

DEVOTIONAL

Develop an attitude of gratitude by recognizing and appreciating God's blessings in your life. Take time to thank Him for His provision, guidance, and grace, acknowledging His goodness and faithfulness.

PRAYER

MAIN POINTS

- ○ Gratitude shifts our focus from what we lack to the blessings we have.
- ○ **Cultivating a heart of gratitude brings joy and contentment in our lives.**

Write down three things you are grateful for today. Spend a few moments thanking God for each of them and expressing your gratitude.

Character Strengths

LIke human needs, we all have character strengths. And like human needs, character strengths present differently for each of us.

Social scientists have identified 25 character strengths that all humans have. Each one of us has a unique mix. Understanding and using them can help to improve relationships, enhance wellbeing and help us better manage stress and problems in life.

Wisdom	Courage	Humanity
Creativity	Bravery	Kindness
Curiosity	Honesty	Love
Judgment	Perseverance	Social Intelligence
Love of learning	Zest	
Perspective		

Justice	Temperance	Transcendence
Fairness	Forgiveness	Appreciation of beauty and excellence
Leadership	Humility	Gratitude
Teamwork	Prudence	Hope
	Self-regulation	Humor
		Spirituality

List your key strengths here:

_____
_____
_____
_____
_____

The Wisdom and Guidance Found in the *Book*

KEY VERSE: _____
_____

"The Lord is my light and my salvation—whom shall I fear? The Lord is the stronghold of my life—of whom shall I be afraid?" - Psalm 27:1

DEVOTIONAL

In moments of waiting and uncertainty, trust in God's perfect timing. Rest in His sovereignty, knowing that He has a purpose and plan for every season of your life.

MAIN POINTS

- God's timing is perfect, and His plans are greater than ours.
- Trusting God's timing allows us to experience His best for us.

PRAYER

Reflect on a time when you had to wait for God's timing in a specific situation. What did you learn about patience and trust during that season?

And finally, equipped with perhaps new or different understanding of yourself, you arrive at the final stage: thoughtful exploration to uncover your purpose.

Work your way through the questions on the following pages. Each of the four questions is presented in a diagram that you can write on. Explore your own understanding on the right hand side, and if it feels right, add the views of people you love and respect on the right.

- Your goal is to come up with answers that feel right, light.
- Remember to have fun - this is supposed to be a life-affirming process for you.
- Enrol your most trusted family and friends - they see you differently to how you see yourself and, usually, they want you to be happy. Ask them to help you answer one or more of the questions.
- Ask as many or as few people as you think are necessary to help you explore the questions.
- Listen closely to their answers - some will be new, much will be what you already know about yourself. If anything makes you feel uncomfortable, allow those feelings to just be.
- Approach this as an adventure, not a job. Experiment and play with the findings. Stretch yourself.
- You're trying to rediscover the small joys of life, the 'you' under the layers of the world's expectations. You're getting to know yourself better than you do today.

Purpose Tracker

Let's deep dive into each of the four Purpose questions. You'll spend one week reflecting on each question.

Track your progress on this page.

Week one - what you LOVE

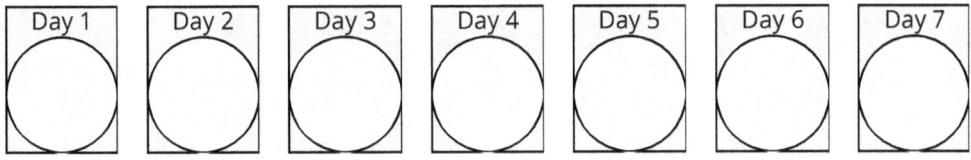

Week two - what you are GOOD at

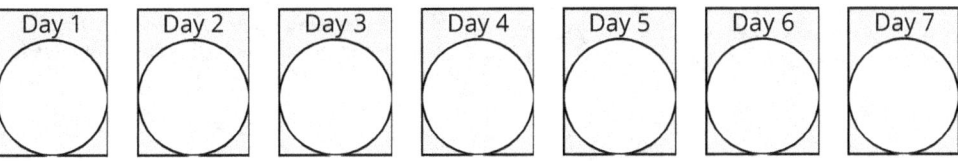

Week three - What the world NEEDS

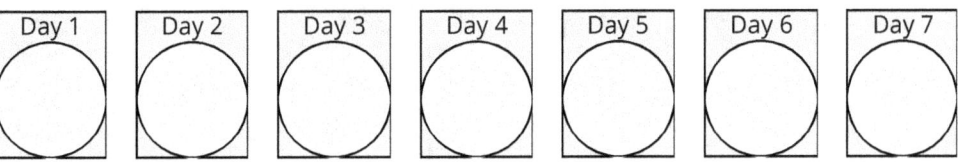

Week four - What you can get PAID for

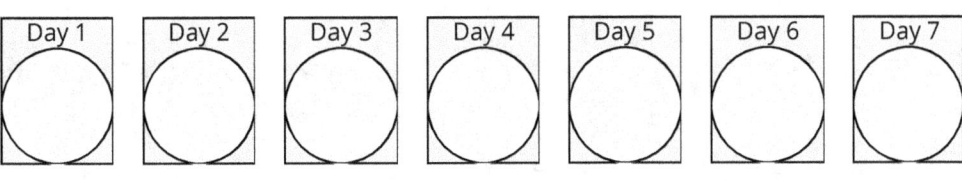

Exploring the Concept of Forgiveness in Scripture

KEY VERSE: _____
_____

"Be strong and courageous. Do not be afraid; do not be discouraged, for the Lord your God will be with you wherever you go." - Joshua 1:9

DEVOTIONAL

Acknowledge your need for God's forgiveness and receive His mercy with a repentant heart. Allow His forgiveness to wash over you, bringing healing and restoration to your soul.

MAIN POINTS

- God offers forgiveness and restoration to all who repent.
- **Embracing God's forgiveness brings freedom and reconciliation in our lives.**

PRAYER

Spend time in prayer, confessing any sins or mistakes you need to seek God's forgiveness for. Meditate on His forgiveness and allow His grace to wash over you.

What Do You Love?

...me things that you can do easily. It might include things you don't like doing but can do easily. The list can include ...ything and everything. The list doesn't need any structure - just write.

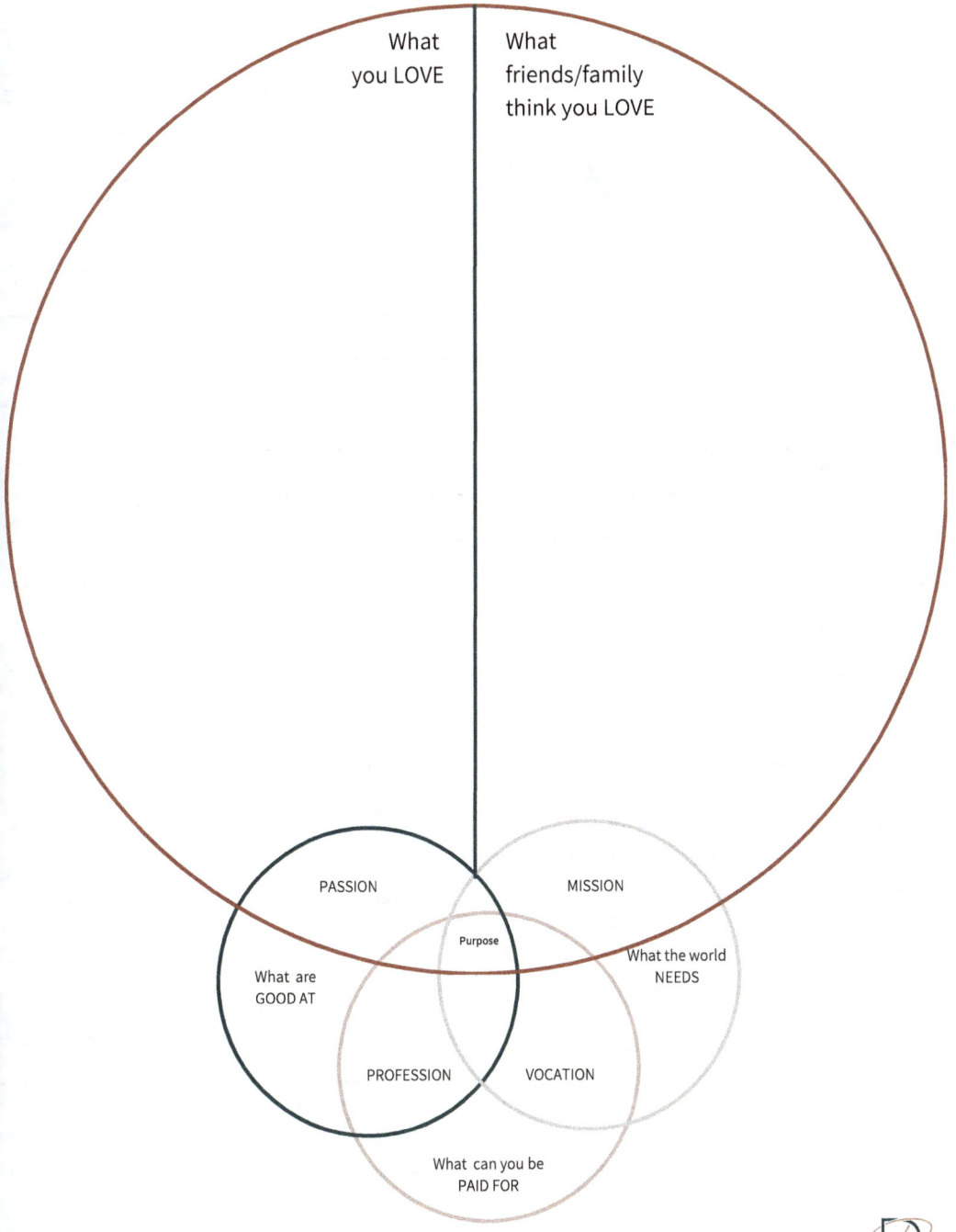

What Did You Learn About What You Love Doing?

"For I am convinced that neither death nor life, neither angels nor demons, neither the present nor the future, nor any powers, neither height nor depth, nor anything else in all creation, will be able to separate us from the love of God that is in Christ Jesus our Lord."
Romans 8:38-39

What Are You Good At?

The things that you can do easily. It might include things you don't like doing but can do easily. The list can include anything and everything. The list doesn't need any structure - just write.

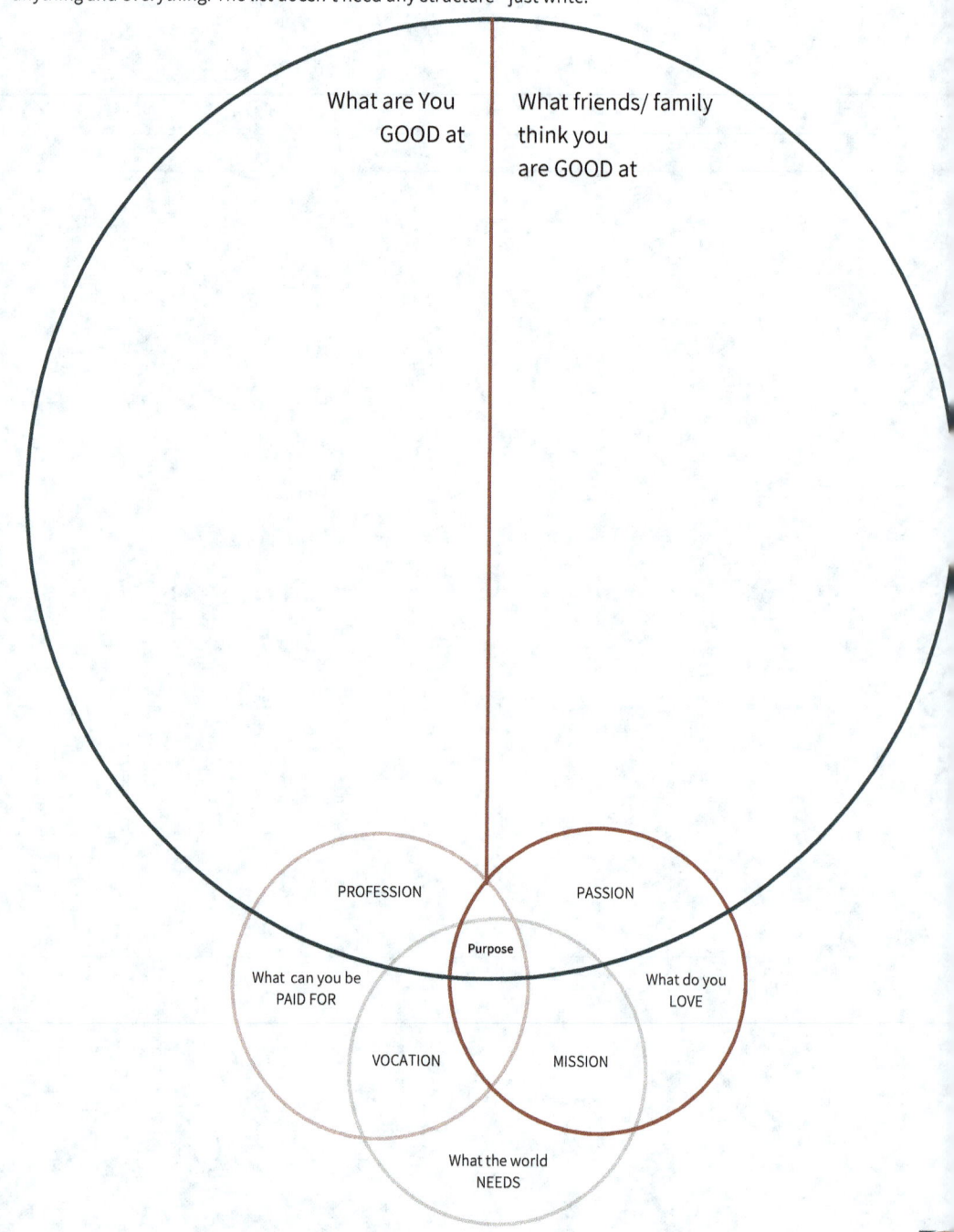

What Did You Learn About What You Are Good At?

What Can You Be Paid For?

The things that you can make money with, that others will pay you to do. You can also think of the rewards you'll get, aside from money. The list can include anything and everything. The list doesn't need any structure - just write.

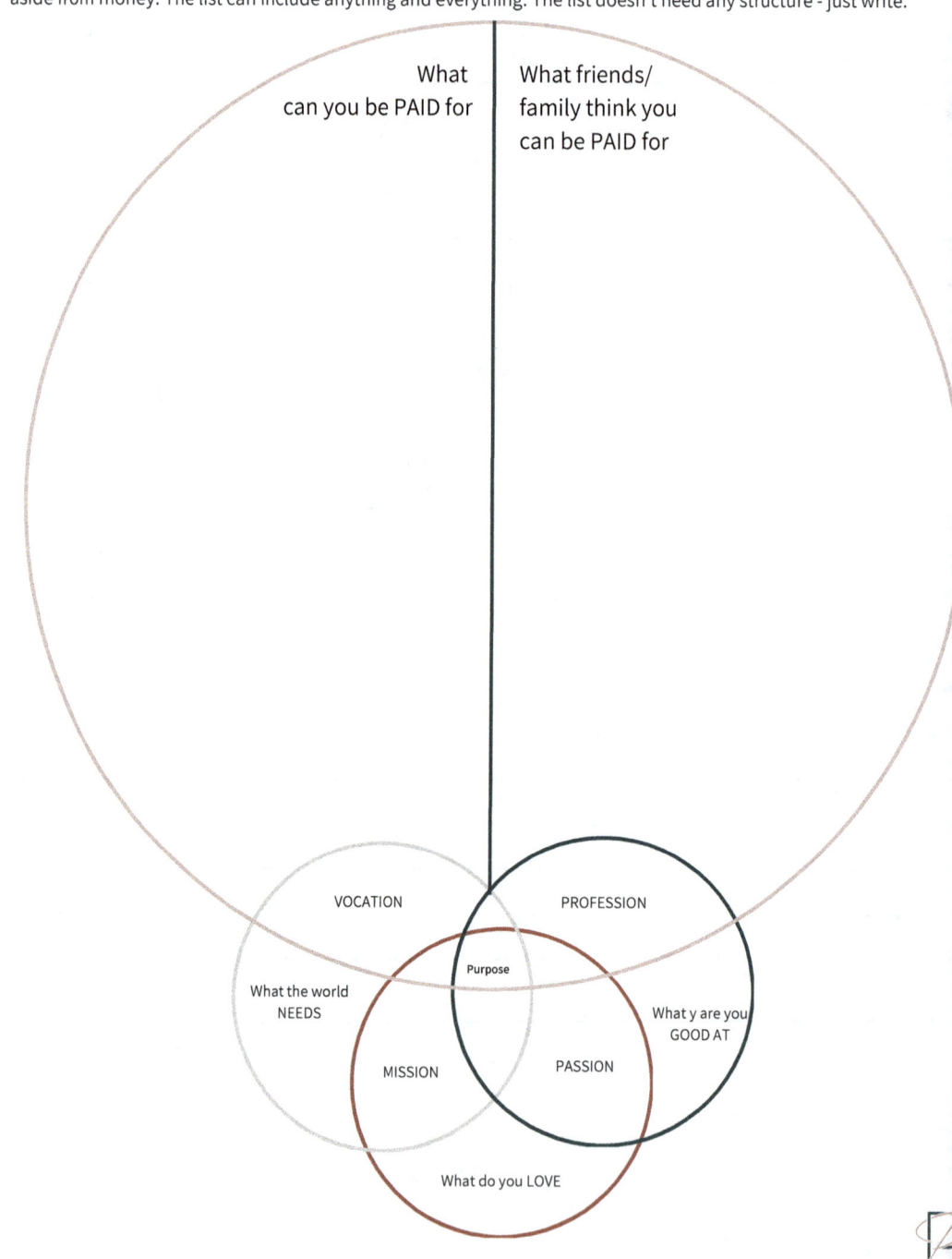

What Did You Learn About What You Can Get Paid For?

"The Lord is my shepherd, I lack nothing. He makes me lie down in green pastures, he leads me beside quiet waters, he refreshes my soul. He guides me along the right paths for his name's sake. Even though I walk through the darkest valley, I will fear no evil, for you are with me; your rod and your staff, they comfort me."
Psalm 23:1-4

What Can You Do To Help The World?

These are things that would help to solve other people's problems. The list can include anything and everything. The list doesn't need any structure - just write.

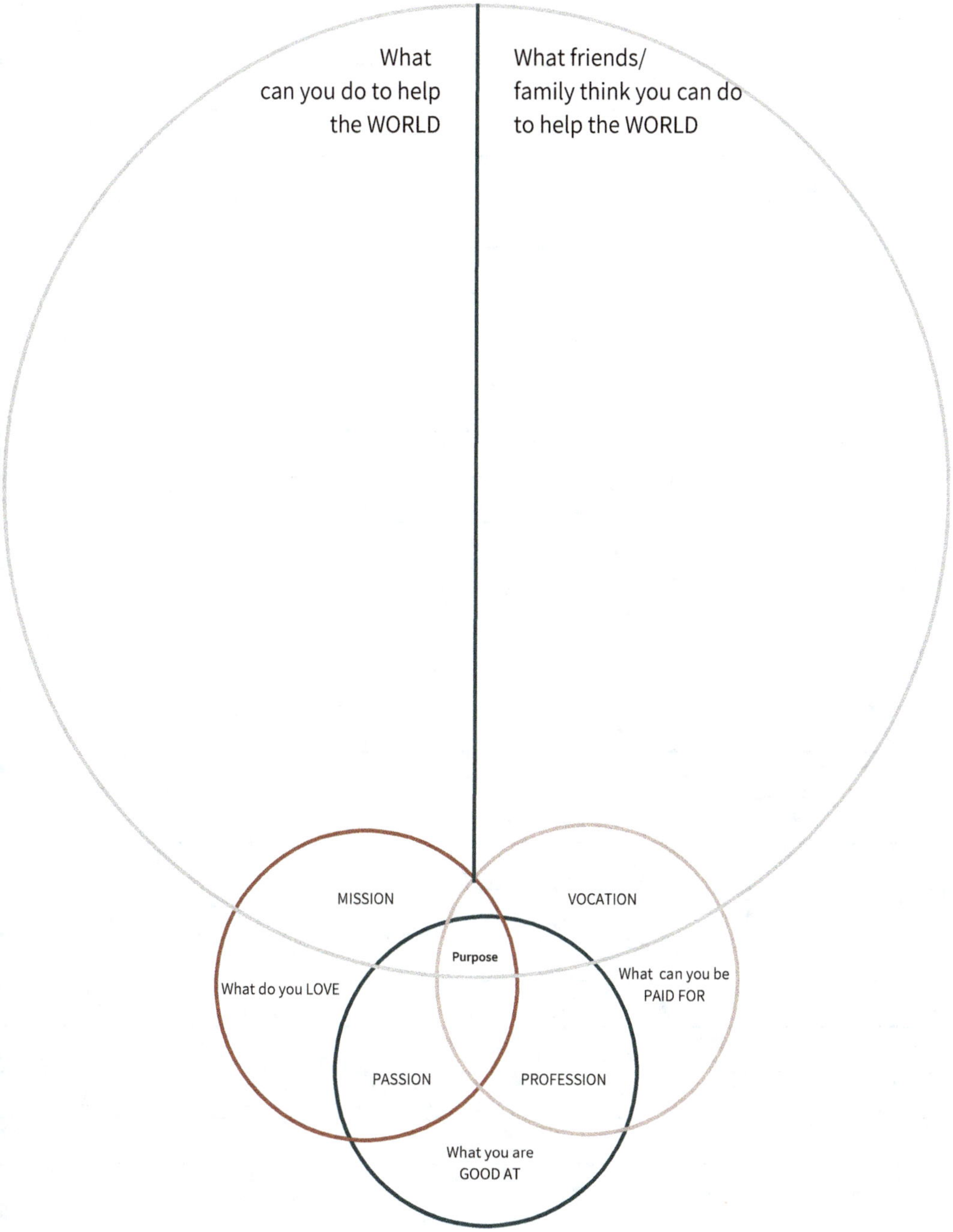

What
can you do to help
the WORLD

What friends/
family think you can do
to help the WORLD

MISSION

VOCATION

Purpose

What do you LOVE

What can you be
PAID FOR

PASSION

PROFESSION

What you are
GOOD AT

What Did You Learn About How You Can Help The World?

Examining the Ten Commandments

KEY VERSE: _____
_____

"Jesus said to her, 'I am the resurrection and the life. The one who believes in me will live, even though they die.'" - John 11:25

DEVOTIONAL

Extend God's love to those around you through acts of kindness, compassion, and grace. Show others the same love and forgiveness that God has shown you.

MAIN POINTS

- God's love compels us to love and show compassion to others.
- Reflecting God's love brings healing and transformation in relationships.

PRAYER

Think of someone in your life who needs to experience God's love. Pray for them and brainstorm practical ways you can show God's love to them.

Finding the Overlaps

Looking at the list on the previous page, which activities overlap?

___

Highlight the one activity that you think is your best choice right now

___

Finding the Overlaps

Why would this be important to you?

How do you think this ties into your key strengths?

My Purpose

"The purpose of my life is to know God and hear his voice so I can live a life of servanthood and obedience; then I will be a God-defined person and a non-anxious presence in every situation."

Is This Your Purpose?

Reflect on your previous page. If you have found your purpose, how does it feel? If you have not yet identified it, how does that feel?

This is How My Life Looks When I'm Living My Purpose Everyday

The Role of Love and Compassion

KEY VERSE: _____
_____

"The fear of the Lord is the beginning of wisdom, and knowledge of the Holy One is understanding." - Proverbs 9:10

DEVOTIONAL

Experience the peace that surpasses all understanding by entrusting your worries and fears to God. Allow His peace to guard your heart and mind in every situation.

MAIN POINTS

- God offers us His peace that transcends all understanding.
- Embracing God's peace brings calmness and stability amidst life's storms.

PRAYER

Write down the areas of your life where you are currently feeling anxious or lacking peace. Surrender each one to God in prayer and ask Him to fill you with His peace.

Action Plan

What steps can you take to make your purpose your focus in your life every day? When will you do each step?

Action step	Date I'll do it

Resources

List the books, podcasts, classes, blogs or people that might help you in your exploration.

You've found your purpose. Now what?

Or perhaps you're close but not quite there. Now what?

At the beginning of this book you read:

Purpose not a life goal to achieve. It is not a framework to measure or test yourself against. It is a daily practice to feel good.

Now it's time to put your purpose into daily practice. Revisit the life vision page from earlier in this book. Add to it.
And start experiencing life living on purpose.

Let's Read, Journal & Pray

Date:

Passage I'm reading:

My reflection of the passage:

Prayer of response:

Notes

IN-DEPTH STUDY

Date:

Passage I'm reading:

Interpretation:
What does it mean?

Re - read text

What do other passages say?

Paraphrase text

What does this mean?

Notes

WRITE THE WORD

Date:

Scripture:

Notes

Let's Read, Answer Questions & Pray

Date:

Passage I'm reading:
_____
_____

My reflection of the passage:

What is God doing in this passage?
_____
_____
_____

How does this change the way I live?
_____
_____
_____

Prayer of response:

Notes

IN-DEPTH STUDY

Date:

Passage I'm reading:

Interpretation:
What does it mean?

Re - read text

What do other passages say?

Paraphrase text

What does this mean?

PURSUING *Purpose*
WITH DR. PEARL

www.PearlPugh.com

www.ingramcontent.com/pod-product-compliance
Lightning Source LLC
Chambersburg PA
CBHW072137070526
44585CB00016B/1712